Folklore

Tim Atkins is the author of *Folklore* 1–25, *To Repel Ghosts*, *25 Sonnets*, and *Horace*. Senior Lecturer in Creative Writing at UEL, editor of the online poetry magazine *onedit*, and translator of Petrarch, Horace, and Buddhist texts, he is a Buddhist, husband, poet, and father. He is a happy man.

Folklore

Tim Atkins

LONDON

PUBLISHED BY SALT PUBLISHING

Acre House, 11–15 William Road, London NW1 3ER United Kingdom

All rights reserved

Salt Publishing 2008, 2011

Printed and bound in the United Kingdom by Biddles Ltd, King's Lynn, Norfolk

Typeset in Swift 9.5 / 13

ISBN 978 1 84471 419 3 hardback
ISBN 978 1 84471 898 6 paperback

1 3 5 7 9 8 6 4 2

to Koto & Chiaki Atkins
All love all

Acknowledgements

Folklore 1–25 was published by Laird Hunt's Heart Hammer Press in 1995. This book in its present form, if at all, would not exist if not for him. Eleni Sikelianos wrote an introduction to that volume and has been a friend and fellow traveller long & ever since.

In various stages and states, Thomas Evans and Peter Jaeger have been generous readers and advisors.

Folklore is for them.

Folklore

One sommers when the soft sonne
Dressed in a shepherds shroud
Went wide in the world for wonders to hear

But on a May morning upon the Malvern Hills
Fell into a vision

The Vision Of Piers Ploughman

I can never forget the effect, a few years afterwards, in England,
of a mountain, in the Malvern Hills. I used to watch them every
afternoon, at sunset, with a sensation which I cannot describe.

— BYRON

1.

Man walks in to sky. Crows, a muttering, didicoy.

Lays his feet in the rain. Tar paper peeling & waters form. His piss blades. The bramble hedge. Crawls through doors. Feathers fall over. His black suit. Lies inside. His dark song.

In his heart he. Lifts the car off the farmer and ran. Tossed his bike in the hedge & wrestles a man down. Ate the flowers with his bare hands.

Rain & rain from the west and the clouds in the shape.

Where you from boy? He says he comes. Says he comes from the borders, boy. He says he comes from Eardisley. Where you from, boy? Where you from?

2.

Breathes in the dry light & dries him. Aspires towards dark.

All the quick animals. The angry the secretive ones.

What are their names? What are their marks?

3.

When he stood up he knocked him back down and the cold.

All night in the lane in the hedgerow lays. Drinking.

His breath it comes out of the man like in sheets, like. Water frozen inside the boots. Sees starlings take sustenance from the earth and circle. Black things come. Before the eyes. Walked for days.

They cuts the small tree and they lay it down. In a line. Like a cut to the neck, half across. So the thing lives and clean. So it flowers. Birds inside too sometimes men. Found a man inside once sleeping. With snow on.

Feels the poplar with his teeth, and the birch. Makes its paper sweet. Where the tongue &. Black branches drip. Water percolates in. Singing. The clear night is in. Stars burn. & waters burn. Watches the light behind the eyes.

Comes into us. Sleep. The Animals sleep. Sucking it down through a straw. The animals sleep. Dies. Every time.

Makes a hedgerow, thus.

4.

Steals between the honeycomb wire and breaks their necks every one. Sees the cold dawn sees it coming up over Bredon's cold hill. Halfway up the nostrils and into fox lungs. Climbs it up and leaves a red stain on the hill side there.

Goes over the fields. Goes over the fields. Like,

5.

Opens the door and the catch pops. Then reaches in for the key. The left hand reaching in. Told me the thumbnail was broken by a bailing machine we seen in a museum—that nobody knows.

Reaches in for the key and finds the key. Feels the cold brass on the fingers ball. The brass shaft and flat teeth of course. In the shape of a crown. Holds the key out and down. Finds the hole in the face in the dark and its ticking tick. Puts it in.

6.

In the pond skimmers' waters. They go down. Comes round the
wrists then the cold eats you there, like the truth she said,
Consumes you. Spring waiting. Summer rolls off the water and
it comes it comes. Into the fields. Made only for eyes. In the
eddies of water where. The gaps between atoms.

Unfolded my sex there, with questions. Beneath this tree.

Thunderflies line the shelf. Like black indians.

When we shoot. The birds fall.

My secrets are.

7.

Life is boundless. Sun.

Was in this barn where. Where the night. Where the night lifts itself up & becomes a sad thing that walks walks like Jesus. Like Jesus in the fields. He places his hand on the machine and the night &. Is not wanted there. Night will be filled now without him.

This machine.

Inside night's clover. Beauty is. (But) it comes there.

Swifts circle the owl's house. But the owl is. Let down. If you break open her pellets, she reveals. Fieldmice, shrews. Voles even are buried there. In her eyes.

So we walk and the dirt road ends there. Suddenly. Why she stops and she cries.

Beneath the purple eaves. Light escapes through the cracks. To be lost there. Night lifts itself up and covers us until there is no air.

Where we were climbed there and her skin was all off & the flowers inside. Breathed in what & out silver. Pollen. Hay-seed. Smeared the dust in our lungs. Paints it all in. Before there was no air there. Inside.

The moon is so empty now. We have left us with nowhere to go. Kissing is.

For good health wear bird's bones. In your clothes.

When you see a falling star, say—

8.

She woke early & feed the child. Warmed her hands over
the ring and light up. Looks out the window at the gorse and
small buildings. Peed and feels its heat rise then back. To the
kitchen heels. Feed the child, Chiron the Healer. Virgo's, no,
Sagittarius's sign.

Lived in a cave and could not die. Had the power to heal others
& knew salves and herbal lore. Administered to all who sought
but could not heal himself. Finally died to allow Prometheus
entry into heaven.

She feed the child, plastic bottle on the plastic table. Robins
fight off & their territory. Sparrows. These warring birds.

Must be lying a couple of hours there and before. Train miles
up the track. How we lay pennies on the rail to stretch them
see. So she must be. The paper says.

Venus with Pluto and so. Hair blowing back down the tracks.
Walking into our face. Because of the planets the paper. She
blows into her hands to keep them warm, this morning, to
keep them warm.

The birds in the tunnel. Forget. Fly straight in and not come
back out again. Black birds, brown birds, red ones. Sleep in the
roofs and eat smoke. From the old trains from Ledbury. Where
the queen. In a bath chair.

Only I remember her. This day. To allow Prometheus to
allow. Because of Pluto of Venus. The day she died in.
Who? Who? What?

9.

Exits without darkness, without light.

When the horse chestnuts blossom in May. The clock comes to measure it by. Songs. Under gates. Walking uphill at an angle. Were fatherless & so. Disappointment's cars.

Bullets drift. Down from an open window. Hanging out. Burning sheets then crying all night. Entered her body. & came out the other side. This cry. Puddles of moisture around her arms. Salt. The memory of. Petals on the shelf. Beneath the sealed up window. Light falling from the tower. "It was."

A passage through glass, through a season. "Look at this little earth." When the body drifts it flys. Flys to the mountain & it. It ascends the path of the stars. It ascends this path of stars called the

Via Latica. (Called) the Milky Way. When the body. When the body dies it is. Gone in June. It is so cold there is even

Cold in the dog.

Gone in June.

10.

Petals fall off the blossom then. What mark to make? Of
beauty? Petals drop from the blossom and bloods come.

It wakes up in the night and does not—Remember her name.

"Tell me." "Tell me your name." "Brown."

All the creatures of the air cannot take this away. Climbs up
the cancer tree. Then builds to a flame.

Loves the water but fears it. Without dreams. Sings full.

Salmon in the river, uncaught.

I (that) remember the teeth of your hair, sometimes.

11.

The organs. Light falls. From the Comet Kohoetek. From

Malvern. Stares into. The night sky.

Pylons.

Plates of rain.

12.

Marches. Dreams, vague shapes. Bubbles caught under. The
first flowers after. This long winter. With no sun on. Either
parents or children. Stirs. In the dawn. All the breath it falls
out. In the hedge. Of the body. & lies green on the floor.

Draws the knees to the chest. Grey spider. How could so much
heat? Do the eyes go out first? Or the light?

Spring waits in. The cold ear. Catches the bird.

13.

Already the eyes. Cannot distinguish between adjectives. Anger requires cranes. Too much eyesight. Looks like stars.

Stares between rooms. Letters in the breath. Large & blur. Towards books.

No object can express its independence. In the lanes between Castlemoreton and Druggers End.

Set out on a journey.

Like a noise in the ear.

14.

Sees raindrops in the air and flies between them. Bees and all.
Women. Or. The insides of gilly-flowers. The chestnut's white
cone. Jasmines. Card side. Climbs down the neck and takes
her pollen takes it. Flies in a straight line & hides her insides.
Covered in honey, pollen, comb. Is a language if.

This mouth built her. All the teeth frames its paper. Talking
swarms—you were—Holding your breasts in your hands for
the stings. How they swarm in all. Bleeding. Gone dark with or
poison. As all falls to the floor.

Liquids lost in the body (sleeping) creatures dream of you.
Dream of you.

Your black pins.

15.

On the corner of. Flowers shut, gates. The spiders make. Comes
out of & catches.

Hymns inside. Webs from the body.

Lies there. In the twilight. Hovers. Gloaming.

Put your hand out the window and the warm wind lines.

Against the warm stones. The air inside my fingers.

Between your ribcage and breast.

16.

I lie in the fields and watch. The grasshoppers grass. Tobacco
the tail makes. Bitter on the tongue. The clouds make a dog's
face. France. An old man with a pipe.

Split grass in the fingers and blew. An acorn cup. Whistles with
the fingers inside. Owl sounds. And steeple. High I and its echo.
Inside & around in the field I sing. How many things.

One day lay there and saw ghosts wrapped round the house.
Like wool. Sometimes one memory. Sometimes a string.

17.

Oils fall from the water. In chromes. Over the dial. To the left,
to the right. Pulls the hair from the face,

The aerial summer.

18.

Smears her back with soft fruits. Love in its traditional. In a different field. Cider is the fruit of. Making love.

Catches flies between her teeth.

The way to obtain pleasure is.

A pronunciation like a lisp like the wind.

19.

The sold priest in the fields. Smells of mildew and rust.

Tewkesbury, Monmouth, Warwick, Burton. Torches walks.
Burns it up.

Yellow cowslip all over the meadow graveyard & common.

Eats an apple in the cold growing cold. Milk fills the skin & falls
out.

Dusk. In church singing. Spitting out pips.

The first day I greased her. Bitter kings.

20.

All week they screw in the yellow bulbs red ones. Round in
their hands. All the morning & talks. Saw them driving geese,
the chicken men. Down from market. Greys and then orange
beaks. The sound of their feathers. The heat inbetween. Holds a
goose egg still warm. Electricity all over the May Fair. The lights
on the cobbles.

You walks & breathe sugar in. Stares into the metal. They
revolve & your teeth ache. Yellow lights make you sick.
Footsteps on the uneven street. Wood and its stuccoed walls.
Perspiration running down. The boys they all. Come down the
street towards the wall of death all for fights &.

All I have is a hand. Coin passing from.

The big wheel arcs over and over the house & chained library
&. Comes for you round & behind then the city. The little lights
narrow. The wrought iron steel, below. Above them then.
Castor & Pollux. The noise of the pump organ goes. Over the
fields & houses & out. Rows then cells settle then darkness oaks
and the black bluff of Hay. Black behind black then. Farewell to
all stars.

Tongue in my tongue. It comes up on the wheel. Hanging out
of our fingers. The cherry paint flakes. Ringing round. The
drawn daggers hit cards. All from here. 3 through the heart's
mark. Steer into each other's legs & the waltzer & on off &
on. The darts diamonds hearts. The wall of death steals. Our
breaths. One more time.

Hit a fox on the road. Halfway home. The lights go up dancing
and after.

Inside the darkness, colour.

21.

Her back broke. A wet axle. At the thousands of grass

If there is no line between. The limbs laying flat, & all.

Worcestershire. Sparking.

In head.

22.

Milks. Stitched into history.

Breaks on the plain.

Walked. From out of.

Places. His.

Hand to the ear.

Hears a man.

23.

The shadows on trees. In the green.

Sun through my sleeve, my body of lawn, my autumn. Stares
over the plain. The alluvial plain. Catch the sound off the swift.
Of the fighter plane. The colt knows her. Concord. Let us not
speak. She—Lies in the grass, she rides on the wild. Rose. In
the eye, in the eye, she lets you—here—

Open her dress. Thunder in the evening, perhaps.

The sky is pouring out of the day of the night,

No label is convincing.

24.

Will the day's journey take the whole long day? The seas in my
ear, the Severn. The answer. Of birds horns.

Awake on the hill on the crest until. The hards gather, dawn.
Unties her from the broken boat & sails over. These fields. If
there was no wind would the leaves? You say.

The veins of the acorn, the alder. What kind of a question?

Walking through the empty field—pacing it off.

The taste of light will always be on your tongue.

25.

Martens on the paper pole, tongues, where do they go?

A reel, a mosquito, in my hand,

and broke it.

26.

Sleep was. Her back of the hills on her side. A room with a
corner. Nails. Staring into her dress. Or just saying there. If I do
this (Jesus) will you? Ask.

If I put my head under the water where does the ocean
go? Will you take a picture of me there? On the ledge? Or the
sun? This. For the branch of the plum and the arc of the back.
Local names of the daisy.

Light inside the legs. Is locked in. All the juice running down.
Forever. The branch paper flakes & holds. The leaves of the
sycamore. Spin down. Finally. Kissing on the mouth. Flies.

Jumped out for the arced branch. It all

Flies. Out.

Okay, I will tell you everything.

Ever and over.

Never.

27.

Feet covered. In hay-fever. Tied to bones.

A gears is. Anyone's

Guess.

28.

The down of her hair. In bubbles less worldly things. Voices
spinning in the river.

Hiding leaves and letters there. In shoots in bracken. My eyes
underneath. The dark leaves rich tips. (Then) the fields swim
out animals insects beneath the hot glass. Burned red money
spiders on concrete, on virginia creeper—

Centuries back—that was it—Insects—reading the Poets of
The Late T'ang.

In the stairs.

Swim, swimming out beneath the hot glass.

Cloistered inside the black spine.

29.

Looking into the world. From this position.

Rails, wants to, but

30.

When he falls it is like the world. Must be made from the absolute.

The brain is a delicate wind that surrounds hinge.

   Hit The Earth.

31.

Cheese of the long river, the wind (gold) of earth. Flowerheads
heads in the garden. Hill covered with pistols.

Had day enough. For love. At this point among many. There
is—nothing random. In a tree—

What love is. The colour of a dog.

Black ants round the hole. Turning. Night on my windows &
legs.

32.

Bells over the water beasts. Trees like a boats. The lime hawk
book. Names from a moth. Springs.

Lies in the stars with his fingers, autumn. With his brown H &
a candle in. Puts it into his foot. Draws it over the flame. The
corkscrew curls. Where the dropper drops. Lets the lights &
the bloods come—before the churn owl picks up his weird his
spinning-wheel song.

Nods when she died, before. Sees her sitting there. On the
post on her bed. A yard bird called dusk. Cried often but did
not listen. With his fingers. Lies in bed & dinosaurs. Makes her
shape on the walls. Believes—

Cockchafers chased under the oaks and the ghost-moths in
meadows. Insects in out of the body,

The caterpillar's green horn.

Folklore. Sonnets. To Repel Ghosts. This and this.

33.

August. 3 peaches

In a dish and a green light

Over Worcestershire

34.

Made him lay in the road. Hid my money in him there & he
always said nothing.

Even when. I hid my money in him he said. Nothing.

Saw horses in a field of rape.

A line in the night. Spun in circles. Said.

I'll do that, Sir, he said. I'll do that.

Falling through the field through the field to the next field.

35.

Inside the heavens. Beings multiplied.

White clouds in the mirror. Always the river.

Sleeps in the wall. Rocking.

His back. Her small hands.

Made him. Swallows. Stones. Map of all bodies.

The lights in the house. On the hill before dawn. The lights round the tree. The mother of father of

This pencil, this pearl,

Makes bargains with insects, with trees. On his back says, if I do this. A will. Am—

A lick inside night —One minute was autumn.

36.

The lights on (their thin bulbs), no light coming out. Stands in the rain raining out, windows gutters. Took him and rubbed his knees into the wet road. (Leaves) his eczema, red flakes on the concrete. Swings up his fist until it finds the teeth bright. Runs him around and around till the eye corners tore. Puts his head between the knees. Drills a hole in the autumn, pulls the skewer up with the pulp. Holds it hanging in the rain. The wet day. Kneels in front of the oven. Calls out.

37.

Times form over the trees. In the east. Makes the myth of
them song. Who cuts roads with their hands. Legions working
towards north.

Strings blackbirds together & makes them. Drink this cup of
electricity. Caractacus. Walks in circles. Before glass.

Sweats for stars. Before they turned into. The crooked plough.
A bought fork. Its disperse. Moving through sky. Towards
perfection. Or perfection. Sometimes crying.

Out of night, the flash of gold. Lashed to the post & carried. To
Rome in chains. Caractacus,

Only a word of love, you understand.

38.

Lists of flames on the leaf. Boxes of apples sheets. For an
instant. In the distance says.

Appears behind hills. Yellow in mist. Her dark hair in plaster.

& at stands. In pipe.

All her beads. Or winters.

It buries the dog,

A lost hand.

39.

In the final light. Hanging. Emerald with duckweed. Under the
sky, light hunting. Known animals. Copies. Their voices with
sounds. Ties their ankles to grass. & in it. Trees, river's run.
Masters the sound of evening sun down.

For epilepsy, a decoction made with flowers of Lavender,
Horehound, Fennel and Asparagus roots, a little cinnamon.

A, B, C, D, E, F, G.

But the screech of the barn or the white owl is often

Often beyond

(his) vinyl

mimicry.

40.

Stalks of onions seed the field. A car's yellow light.
When the weather. Peels back the wind. Inside fields, runs.

Up the roads. Throws a stone through the woman. Looks but
does not remember. Their names. A girl in braids a left tin.
A collection of something, a Woman. Walked this way only.
Once. From Kington.

He peels the label. In the moon. Clover behind the photo. A
gone one. Circles down.

Glasses of crack, Romany.

Lives. Perhaps worn behind the ear.

41.

The knuckles of fingers

Drives into light.

A trees hair is.

Wings fall.

42.

Two crows flying. Written on the back of. Always as love, dropped plums, things. Being nothing they couldn't see. All lives. In the field's whistle. Looks the dream in the eye sees it. Walks in the direction.

Sunlight in the smell of light from the empty lane. Grass grows between.

Summer was. A plastic bag in a tree.

43.

Climbs the flagpole greased. Speaks. Hides, stays there. Forces
himself into the blue yellow blue bell of the crocus body.

This. Boy. After a twisted man. This

Arm is a stream. Measured against the doorpost.
The animal runs.

Every creatures. Tries. Nights in an envelope.

44.

At the end of summer pass on knowledge by tongue. &
dancing. Her substance. Is this. Apiary. In this way grow to
know she is good to her too.

To be with her & work & to know that she is in good health.
These small women works.

A substance from her skin also prevents the ovaries from
developing.

Looked into the paper tree and saw.

His mother young again.

45.

Speaks but the days swallows night. Where. All voices look like
nothing.

From twelve till light. It—Grains. Through the ear. Through
the bird. The blue chair. A heard falling. & no promised. Comes.
But a night.

Taking off. The light behind. The Colds. Suns. Spectrums not
seen. Through the eye's essential oils.

Or do the eyes go out first?

46.

Stalks separate from the plant body, the capillaries of leaves. Grass falls on grass. Cants in water.

Fires across the coin. Elements move through. Conkers—from conquer. Her coats sold for daughters.

Water fills. Wipes its face. Licks her thumb. A womb built of mud. This always was.

Fell into sleep by the roadside. Holding this book. Leaves.

Syllables break off in the wind.

47.

Along rails, sloes in the river clays, inhabits roses, limestone.

Attains the quality of black granite, honeys dust, dripping
spring. Approaches heights, remembers Raggedstone,
Midsummer. Names of the hills. Rivulets running off lights. In
lines in the rain. Nights in the stone. Lays down under. Drives
all day. Across the summer lands

Stars spread out over Wales. Towards Hay. Listens to their
strange voices, stands at the piano singing, lingers in the
marketplace. Gauges the quality of. The placenta in grass dark.
The weathered bones. Pulls up among winter.

Bangs in the piano. A motion.

Dips in the branches. Spreads her legs.

Chalks. Sex, sex again.

48.

She reads to Andromeda. In the corners, it, falls. Leans back &
shows her left shoe,

Information forks.

49.

Clear water in a glass. Enters the mouth through the ear.

She unpins her leg and leaves it on the Severn. Climbs beneath.

50.

Lives in their intricate movement. Days in watches & insides of stones.

Mossed Agate. Tiger's Eye. Carnelian. Jet. Wearing The Jeweller. Repeating their names.

Cries in the chains. What makes me? What makes him? Lock the shop.

Hand rested. On guns. Its ticks. He/she—

Stands in the corner. Soaping the black hairs under her armpits.

Words words.

51.

In the painting. Of St Wulstan's. There is black & blue. Blue & blue. Black. Lithium. Inside mistletoe. & When he disappears. The saint hesitates.

This intermittent. This speaking, is. Handkerchiefs inside grains of salt. Blinding. Like a necklace. In the green woods.

Binding.

52.

In his hands. Pages soap. Masons. Thick with impassable. Slates.

This warm fall. Bodies coughed in the floods. Cow with its current form. At the thin end of breath.

At this turning, at this corner. Working forms. Intuition. Over the rutted road. Beneath the fathers. Shrouded in fog.

Hovers but not. The solicitors judge. Plugs of tobaccos cars. Visits. Salts. Nailed into their tongues. This silence is. An incredible handshake. Crows. Can't tell the difference. Where police sleep on the straight.

They. Lost the position. Of the apostrophe. Where they all can.

Do this.

Plan escape.

53.

Wakes in. A plum stone.

Speaks into tables. With a handful of signs. Lays them on the same. Dreams of. Mends fences.

Breathing, sighing is a sign.

54.

Spits from whistling. All that was. In the hand. Learned from.
Stitching. Her scars.—When she sung.

Stares into his heart leaves. & closed it. Placing the arrow in his
eye. Locking limbs.

The car couldn't. Understand. A blue fly in the moon. Shining.
Its pissed winds. As a vehicle for movement. Motions into the
organs. Filled with blood.

This prison. A brother long. Forever. Made of. Homes. Heads.
Towards Hereford. Hereford.

With broken teeth.

Almost gone.

55.

And after he wandered. Like a real soldier
& came off the train
& surrendered with his legs
& was sent back

The vicar wrapped his eyeballs in
Bunting
& at every parade

Cuts off the ears. Makes a chain.

56.

Copper enters. A pair of oils. Then the acids. Etch monies. All
they showed. From the outside. From the street. Was a window,
a door.

If this is no training. Then what is? The notes on a table.
Keeping the fire in. Clouds passing over. As if peppered to
walls.

The riches of winds.

Be apples come autumn.

Her eyes reading this.

57.

Knots. The bowstring. The wood between fingers.

Feathers brushing the arrow's flight. Kisses the eye line. The
nape of. Into the eye socket. At the corner. & lances the tongue.

Summers. Sings from the bow.

Its runs through the brother.

58.

When the body moves to get cool. Fishes swim in. The bones of her. Back.

Meadowfescue. Timothy. Aspirin. On each blade. Towards the smokes.

Towards evening. In & out.

To the last living body.

All the pollens in the world. At this angle. Are falling.

So fast. There is hardly no mark.

59.

The stickleback sleeps. All through. The month of rains.

The night. The heart rolls in.

60.

Lies on his back below. With a star for a nose.

Something about the heart. Suddenly. O mole.

The flowers move and he looks at them.

Shining in the small light. World. Go.

61.

Runs over fields see. Through thickets, copse, water-meadow,
orchards, fallow-fields, ploughed & flood pasture. Over tracks.
Between rivers shout. Its fear. Pulls in its hands. & said tongue
hanging now. At the fall. Axes warrens. A red man picks up the
dead brush & paints himself out. Bloods then. Sets. The horse
dogs call. Over the children's horn. Lives but does not. Sports
foam on a horses all.

A neck winds through the fox bone. Daubed on the shoulders,
face. Perhaps the moaning, perhaps the blood. A palaces,

Their red. Makes me.

Versus, screams. All things.

62.

Set out for & came back with. Hours. Is, is, and is.

Water has no answer.

Our great love.

63.

The soft contours of the oak. The horse chestnut's fine teeth.
Counters of eaves catch in the bonfire light & swim upwards.
Calls them in & sucks them. From the boughs to the pound.

Looks south from the fires limestone. North for Clee Hill and
its break. Rushes out from its centre. The long chain of flames.

Dreams she saw the Armada. Coming. In her box for all day
on or land. Men walking. Decks of wood. In the English water.
She asked then. They build fires. Its light out. For to burn the
brown skin & dark eyes. In all walks. With their rich gods and
cock. Or half useless. Looks out on her land & corns in—

Out from the canopy of trees. The stones in the ditch. The
bottle top. Soft green glass. Asks the fire. To the beacon & back.
In the distance matches manufacture England's Glory & prison.
A black hills in the west. Will later lay flat on this. Will ask it to
take this away. Fire. Stumbles. Stumbles in.

England is lead. Granite rush. Over 400 years old.

Kissed on the teeth. Pith. If you. Ask in the ditch.

The mouth and the earholes, all full.

64.

Red month, I repeat myself. In all Worcestershires. Honey.
Asleep in the rafters sleep. Creaking.

The knuckles of fingers. Drives into night. A trees hair is.
Wings fall.

Which walks beside her. Diaspora Before her. The dor-beetle's
drowsy hum, the onion heads swaying.

See that thing up there? Cathedrals. Raining over the hole.
Heavens, or. Despairs. English frame.

The soul resides in the rust in the hinges hear them.

65.

Clays were the most. Her pelvis kept. In sandy soils. Breaking shape. All rivers run. Into Severn.

Linked by compassion. To other structures. A ring of gold. Was in front of the station & flames. About her virginity, her stomach.

Although it was autumn. Waking in hail. I wanted. To forget the falling leaves. Its essential.

Kisses the sweet earths. Must pass through. Now. Must always.

Love the eye.

66.

The wind in the guttering crimson. Lives. In a bottle. In gins.
Mother. Puts her hands around morning. For leaves & the wake.
Looks into the cup. & it sees. At the leaves there.—Speaking.
Collapses &. Collapses in.

Man puts his knife round the scrotum & cuts off the balls. Its
silver hides. The gold teeth & rings.

Takes a wick of kindling and lays it. Wadding the newspaper
watches the print come off. Damps it down with the fist say
and fires it. Up and over. Smoke from the chimney air. Just like
in the leaves. Over the roads & on, gone. All the smoke crimson
green. Wet arches trained into horseshoes. Drips in the day.
Crumble into nothing. In wind.

Looked for her bones. A day too late to. Listen to her, sing.

She mixes her hair with the man the man's footprints dirt &
burns them. Adds the ashes to his food. Says.

Blood does not clot in a cold a cold wind.

It arches, tins.

67.

Pushes the margins. Journeys.

Always talking. Always falling.

Forever left.

68.

A space ploughed up by the wind. Acorn, Acker. A ripple or dark streak on the surface of water. The same.

Storm passing. Following. Fires in the fields. Purple flowers— Called something. I have no idea.

"Of all that is said in the world—"

Is a volume. A distant city.

Stole this from the ankle. & sent it.

69.

& when he awoke.

The light on the channel

Pears glowing on their trees.

And, now that life had so much human promise in it, they resolved to go back to their own land; because the years, after all, have a kind of emptiness, when we spend too many of them on a foreign shore. We defer the reality of life, in such cases, until a future moment, when we shall again breathe our native air; but, by-and-by, there are no future moments; or, if we do return, we find that the native air has lost its invigorating quality, and that life has shifted its reality to the spot where we have deemed ourselves only temporary residents. Thus, between two countries, we have none at all, or only that little space of either, in which we finally lay down our discontented bones. It is wise, therefore, to come back betimes — or never.

N.H.

CPSIA information can be obtained at www.ICGtesting.com
Printed in the USA
BVOW021252150412

287706BV00002B/2/P